THE FRAGILE PEACE YOU KEEP

For Catherine, Friend, sister & theater companion — May be both continue, side by side, on the road to happy destiny. Love, Kel

THE FRAGILE PEACE YOU KEEP

POEMS

BY KEL MUNGER *Kel Munger*

Minnesota Voices Project Number 88
New Rivers Press 1998

First Edition
Printed in the United States of America
Library of Congress Catalog Card Number: 97-69841
ISBN: 0-89823-186-8
Edited by Debra Marquart
Copyedited by Joanne Fish
Front cover photograph by Rita Cihlar
Book design and typesetting by Percolator

New Rivers Press is a nonprofit literary press dedicated to publishing
the very best emerging writers in our region, nation, and world.

The publication of *The Fragile Peace You Keep* has been made possible by
generous grants from the Jerome Foundation; the Minnesota State Arts
Board (through an appropriation by the Minnesota Legislature); the North
Dakota Council on the Arts; and Target Stores, Dayton's, and Mervyn's
by the Dayton Hudson Foundation.

Additional support has been provided by the Elmer L. and Eleanor J.
Andersen Foundation, the Beim Foundation, the General Mills
Foundation, Liberty State Bank, the McKnight Foundation,
the Star Tribune/Cowles Media Company, and the contributing
members of New Rivers Press.

NATIONAL
ENDOWMENT
FOR THE
ARTS

NORTH
DAKOTA
COUNCIL
ON THE
ARTS

MINNESOTA
STATE ARTS BOARD

New Rivers Press
420 North Fifth Street, Suite 910
Minneapolis, MN 55401

www.mtn.org/newrivpr

For Sheryl Linn Beauvais

CONTENTS

TEN CODES

POEMS FOR THE GHOSTS

RE-MEMBERING

TOURING THE COAST

ACKNOWLEDGMENTS

Poems in this manuscript have previously appeared in the following journals and anthologies: *Appalachee Quarterly* ("The Baker's Helper"), the *Association of Women Students Newsletter* ("Woman Walking Toward Herself"), *Black Buzzard Review* ("The Meatpacker"), *Flyway* ("Ophelia, Diving," "Why the Dog Howls at the Moon"), *Iowa Woman* ("Babi Yar"), *Lesbian Review of Books* ("After Making Love, We Hear Sirens"), *Lynx Eye* ("The Red-Haired Waitress," "Another Guilty Little Poem"), *Periphery* ("Mordecai, In the Sewer," "Rolf und die Apfelsine," "Touring the Coast," "Linslaw Cutoff"), *Sketch* ("Fat Ladies," "What We Had To Do"), and *Sinister Wisdom* ("Re-Membering: The Color of Silence"). "The Red-Haired Waitress" and "After Many Years, Griselda Loses Patience" were published in the anthology *The Muse Strikes Back,* edited by Katherine McAlpine and Gail White (Story Line Press, 1997).

I wish to thank the Iowa State University Department of English for the 1995-96 Pearl M. Hogrefe Fellowship in Creative Writing, which made many of these poems possible. My professors have been indispensable in the development of my writing, and several of them deserve particular mention for their guidance, criticism, and support: Neal Bowers, Susan Carlson, John McCully, Neil Nakadate, and Susan Yager.

A special note of thanks to Bill Truesdale at New Rivers Press for his ongoing encouragement and enthusiasm as this manuscript has evolved. Debra Marquart, editor, mentor, and friend, has been invaluable in her support. Thanks also to Julie Comine, "another damn poet," an excellent critic, and a good friend, for her help with these poems.

In addition, I would like to express my immense gratitude and affection to my commanding officers, Chief Dennis Ballantine, Captain Jerry Snider, Sergeant Mike Becker, Corporal Pete Conis, and Lead Dispatcher/Jailer Jan Stoeffler, for their support and encouragement during the writing of these poems. All of my former colleagues, the women and men of the Ames, Iowa, Police Department, were both supportive and indulgent of poetry on duty, and for that I am very grateful.

I deeply appreciate the spiritual support I received from all my coffee-drinking friends, and from the members of The September 29th Movement.

TEN
CODES

THE POLICE DEPARTMENT'S NIGHT DISPATCHER

. . . Ames, all cars, prepare to copy . . .

The town is not asleep,
it is comatose.
In the quiet, I broadcast
weather reports, just to hear
something break squelch.
I imagine them out there, in the dark.
What do they see
from behind the dash?
Shadows of streets
and not the streets themselves;
the outline of a town,
not quite filled in?

I name the places and numbers
as serenely as possible,
without knowing the color of houses,
where doors and windows open
onto alleys, the placement
of shrubbery and fences. I know
the events: a wife-beater lives
across from the church; the third duplex
from the corner houses an arsonist:
there was a suicide in the garage
behind the school.

My voice is my weapon
in these choppy waters of night,
and when the call goes out,
I know eternity
in the space between arrival
and resolution, in the vast expanse
of seconds and inches
between danger
and safety.

THE ACCOMPLICE

I have in my possession certain information
which may or may not be valuable—
dates, places where particular words were spoken,
though not the written order. No one kept that.
Like the man who sold the bullets, the woman
who took cash for the gas, and the boy
who cleaned the windshield of the getaway car,
I keep my head low, contributing my small part
to the vertiginous spin of fate.
I become that nameless warrior who stepped back
so that Uriah would die, fighting the urge
to ask those who know, those who wave
the bloody stump of their honor as if it were whole—
I want to ask them *why*, and dare not.

10-78/OFFICER NEEDS ASSISTANCE

The fragile peace you keep,
shattered

like the beer bottle he hit you with.
Its broken pieces press
against your damp cheek.

The dark barrel of your own gun
hard against the back of your neck,
blue on blue.

His warm, desperate breathing.

Your warm, desperate breathing.
A trickle of moisture,
blood or sweat, into your eyes.

Wet paving stones
in this sour alley.

You listen for sirens,
hoping they come,

dreading their arrival.

CAUGHT SHOPLIFTING, A BOY RUNS HOME AND KILLS HIMSELF

    First order,
the rows upon rows of bottles and cans
lining the shelves like tenpins
at the end of a hardwood lane.
    Then disorder,
chaos springing from the clerk, the manager,
the swiveling heads of the shoppers
as they turn to stare at you.
Chaos full-grown from your head
like a child of Zeus, chaos clapping
in your ears with the thunderbolt crack
of a new god or your father's four-ten,
    and finally:
what's left here are dull spatters,
the idiot hum of nerve endings, and sirens.

10-79/NOTIFY CORONER

1. The Old Woman

You have died, and the cop is afraid
to roll you over, doesn't want to find a wound.
You want to comfort her, to say
It's all right, I took a bite of muffin and was gone.
She is so pale, so young, as she walks
around your living room, cataloguing the items of your life:
the walnut corner cabinet, full of porcelain pieces,
dainty crocheted doilies lining the shelves,
the sour odor of bacon fried for breakfast,
braided rugs covering hardwood floors,
yesterday's *Tribune* folded open to the crossword puzzle.
This business of dying—it's never simple—
no matter how recently you've dusted and swept,
there are still some things left undone.

2. The Suicide

You have a puzzled look on your face, as if to say
This isn't what I meant, I take it back.
But nothing here gets taken back, it's all for keeps:
yellow tape, red lights, and neighbors
peeking out from their doors, hoping for a glimpse
of the black plastic bag on its gurney.
It takes two people to cut you down—
one holds your body steady, the other mounts
a stepladder and saws through your rope.

They crack jokes about your still-running watch
until the captain silences them with a scowl.
Later, they will all three wake in the night,
shaking, wondering why it was you this time,
wondering why they still breathe as they swing.

3. The Baby

Her tiny lips have gone dark,
like the petals of the most delicate violet,
and even though he knows
it's too late, he opens them with a forefinger
and puffs gentle ventilations
into her silent chest.
Behind him, the hysterical babysitter
screams herself quiet
while the approaching ambulance howls
out grief in the world.

TO THE FOURTEEN-YEAR-OLD RUNAWAY WITH VENEREAL DISEASE

What's odd here is that you still seem like a child at all,
jerked through the station door, walking stiff-legged in pain.
The men see you as a teenage Medusa, turning balls
to stone, and leave you to wait with me while social workers try again.
I bring you food—milk, a snack cake from the vending machine—
and you, so wary, with a white-froth mustache over your shaking lip,
jut out your chin defiant, mutter thanks, then retreat to the sheen
of a juvenile prostitute with both active business and infection, oh-so-hip
to the street, the cops, the child welfare system that fails
again each time you touch it. You pace, you sulk; I wonder
what happens when your cool step falters, your bravado pales?
All I can offer is another round of Ho Ho's against hunger,
a small chocolate-cream gift in your world without peace
where hope has become the most deadly disease.

THE 911-DISPATCHER READS BOETHIUS ON DUTY

For Susan Yager

You would have been a philosopher if you had remained silent.
Consolation of Philosophy

I pick it up on the first ring, my book already pushed aside,
and hear the boy crying, frantic: *Jack's gonna kill my momma!*
followed by an adult roar and the almost-damp thud
of a seven-year-old body striking something solid—
then white noise, crackling, the cord jerked from its wall.
Soon Jack is led, hands cuffed behind his back,
through the metal doors and pushed, belly-first, to the counter.

Reason completes the paperwork, huffs under her breath
and turns the page, stomach grumbling. Here,
in this hungry country of unkindness, I have become
an unwilling philosopher, a *professional*. No screams,
no rage, no howls of indignation—I treat them all alike.
Dispassion masquerades as justice, and no consolation
arrives in this cell to minister to either injured or injurious.

The boy who called for help disappears into the same system
that swallows in greedy gulps all it is offered,
some gluttonous idol of the rational world too briefly propitiated.
Weeks later, I will wake in the middle of the night, out of breath
from my dream of hidden, endlessly ringing telephones,
and I will console myself with chocolate milk, a prayer,
and no philosophy: in this country of unkindness,

what fills the mind leaves the spirit starving.

THE ROOKIE CONTEMPLATES MORTALITY AFTER ATTENDING THE FUNERAL OF A FELLOW OFFICER

Sestina for Officer Todd Gohlmann

From the birth of the world I wore blue,
as if my heart and life were one
with the daytime sky, and the earth
held me steady. Then would I, too,
walk the streets to keep the peace
and shower baton blows on the face of death.

Now I've buried a man who wore a shield, and death
patrols the night shift, its colors blue
as gun barrels, its colors burning away peace.
Each car, each man, perhaps the one
to send me down, face first; me, too,
breathing in the sour, enduring earth.

I took my place to see him safe to earth,
and joined that long, uniformed line marching toward death.
Our dirge was the scattered radio chatter, too
furious to call a drumbeat, lights blue
and red and white, wig-wagging one
color after another on streets without peace.

Packing my oath like an oiled piece,
I pass among the spirits of air and earth,
counting each pace *contra mortem*, one
foot ahead of the other, away from death,
I think, without assurance. Blue
and white blossoms planted in rows of two

abreast line the road, line the path to
the graveyard. We put him down to peace
in a casket with brass handles, lined with blue
silk. Perhaps it will outlast the earth,
perhaps not; either way, all that remains is Death,
the bastard, who cheats even after he's won.

Later, I will try to remember one
face out of the many, two
hands out of the hundreds, that death
did not mark with darkness, with some piece
of the final, resolute earth.
I will try to remember if the wind blew.

One day, shrouded at last in blue, my only shield the one
I wear on my chest, I will be led to earth, too;
I will keep at last the peace of always too-soon death.

THE TURNKEY

I fixed up a padded cell and lugged it around.
I locked myself in and nobody knew it.
Only the keeper and the kept in the hoosegow . . .
Carl Sandburg

There are walls and bars and mesh,
high-impact plastic, unidentifiable metals,
institutional white paint, door handles
on the outside only, and locks.
Plenty of locks.

There are cameras mounted at odd angles
in the corners, tinny loudspeakers
for administering confusion, fireproof mattresses,
single-ply toilet paper, and locks.
Plenty of locks.

Keys are a sort of chain, a link connecting us.
The circular, persistent illogic of the truly drunk
resounds like a held note from Joshua's horn,
knocking down these tempered-steel holding pens:
even the bars cannot separate us.

And if, in the draining fluorescence of the booking counter,
in the unremitting white glare of the cells,
the jailer begins to resemble the jailed,
remember that neither of us is free to leave:
locks make prisons, locks make prisoners.

WHAT COPS KNOW

The odd, wet sound, so like a gourd
against the pavement, that a boy makes
when his body is slammed against a wall.

The color of panic, alternating red and blue
as the cyclical flashing of take-down lights, reflecting bruises
on the face of a crying woman.

And the molten, coppery scent of blood on tile,
so that the kitchen where the corpse rests
smells hot and airless as a foundry.

Most of all, we know the shape of secrets,
the power of a gaze that makes everyone
look away, even those who are guilty

of no crime they know, no crime we can name.

WHAT COPS DON'T KNOW

He can tell how old the tracks in the snow
around a building are, how long ago those pry marks

on the door were made, and with what tool.
He's faced down a man with a gun, tackled a fleeing shoplifter,

been hit head on in his squad car by a driver too drunk
to see the flashing lights. He's rescued a cat from a burning house.

I've *heard* that he can see in the dark—he never takes the flashlight
out of its dashboard mount when he goes stalking a prowler.

He saunters into the squad room on this June afternoon,
looks at the news on cable TV, shakes his head violently.

I can't stand queers! he says, and takes a seat
at the briefing table, right next to me.

AFTER MAKING LOVE, WE HEAR SIRENS

. . . Two women sleeping
together have more than their sleep to defend.
Adrienne Rich

Here in the center of town—one block
from the fire station, two blocks from the hospital,
four blocks from city hall, where I work
in a steel and bulletproof glass-encased police station—
we hear sirens all the time. Yet, for some reason,
they seem most likely to sound—not while we are cleaning,
eating supper, playing with the dog, reading quietly
at opposite ends of the couch—but at moments like these,
as we lie side by side, naked, whispering,
singing stupid old songs to each other.
Light from the hallway spills into the room,
glints on the badge I've left atop the dresser
in the dust neither of us has time to wipe off.
I remember the first time I pinned that badge
to my uniform shirt, carefully centered my name tag
over the right chest pocket, went off to keep the city safe.
It was what I'd wanted forever, until I wanted you.
In another city, another state, loving you might be a crime—
and then what badge could I wear, what justice for us,
what sirens would we listen for?

POEMS FOR THE GHOSTS

BABI YAR

(Kiev, 1941)

1.

The sky was brittle blue above us,
like the rims of the dairy dishes my mother kept,
and winter seemed ready to crack and shatter
as we marched, line after ragged line, into the wooded hills.
An old woman walking ahead of me kept stumbling,
her delicate, ancient feet catching on the frayed hem
of her black dress; finally, she fell.
I knelt to help her up—she took my hand without apology,
as if to comfort me. *Walk beside me, grandmother,* I said,
and carried her fragile bones like a picnic hamper
on my arm until we came to the forest.

2.

At first, I thought I'd wakened in her arms,
but there were so many arms around me.
I breathed deep the fertile scent of moss
as it began to grow along the crease of my elbow.
The damp earth wrapped around me like a blanket
knitted of the blood and urine and tears of all of us,
lying there, in a trench in a Russian wood.
She took my hand, squeezed tight my fingers in her palm,
held me breast to breast until death passed.
Then our bodies fell away, and I was comforted.

MENDEL THE SNATCHER

(Warsaw, 1942)

I'm *quick,*
with hands that pop
like rifle fire.
My eyes are shiny stones
to throw at soldiers.
I stalk little gray air-people
who clutch their packages
against them, tight as fists.
But I'm *quick,*
I snatch and gobble as I run,
sliding through low holes in the Wall.
I dig like a badger
through the Pole's garbage,
and run back fast.
Once, I got caught halfway through the Wall
and soldiers beat me from both sides.
But I'm *quick,*
I got away, and snatched
some dry noodles for dinner.
I'm hungry again.
I duck down an alley
and head for the Wall,
but there are Black Shirts
at the cross street.
They're *quick,*
and one shot
snatches me
from the world.

MORDECAI, IN THE SEWER

(Warsaw, 1943)

1.

I'm hungry, but that's all right;
a tight belly is no stranger here.
For weeks, all the food we had was a carter's horse;
not kosher, but even Reb Elias ate our stew.
You laughed at him, Dov, and said
>   *When this is over, I'll paint pictures*
>   *of rabbis eating ham sandwiches.*
But it's not over, not yet.
Two nights ago, you touched my shoulder,
whispered *Masada.*
Dov, I saw you die this morning,
saw a machine gun you'd stolen
from the partisans explode
in your artist's hands.

When we were students, you told me
>   *If we are to survive individually,*
>   *we must die as a people.*
But, Dov, you died a Jew,
screaming the first prayer you ever learned
as those damned soldiers raked you
with their perfect weapons.

2.

It must be late;
the light filtering through manhole covers

is a much deeper purple than when we began.
I'm thirsty, Dov.
Waist-deep in this thick water,
my throat's as dry as the Sinai.
If I should drink . . . around me, bodies hang on the barbed wire
        those fornicating Germans strung down here, bodies
        already bloated and decaying . . .
I won't die in this damned cesspool!
Dov, you bastard, I'm a poet,
not a soldier; I'll choose another end,
one with honor.

3.

When we were boys,
we were expelled from school twice
because you kept challenging the teachers
and I was always listening to you.
Finally, your father taught us at home,
laughing at us, calling us "David" and "Jonathan."
        Remember yourself, you wrote,
        because the rest of the Jews
        will remember everything else.
Dov, the walls are getting lower here,
closer to the top, closer to the edge
of this decomposing city. And, Dov, my friend,
damn you for dying, and damn me, too—
because I intend to live.

ROLF UND DIE APFELSINE

(Treblinka, 1943)

1.

they march past me everyday
vainly covering their wrinkled genitals
with skinny gray hands
as if I wanted to see a hairy Jew's cock
I smile

later I hear them tearing at the walls
with their fingernails
it squeaks like a chalkboard
scratched by schoolboys

Heinz has a watch
so we place bets on how long it takes
for a roomful of smelly kikes to die
not very damn long

at the end of the day
we must go into the chamber
and supervise stony-eyed *Sonderkommandos*
as they resurface the walls
it smells like oranges

2.

we bake bodies like bread
crusty Yiddish *schwartzbrot*
like we used to buy on Gröningstrasse

when neither Heinz nor I had money
we'd waylay the baker's son
as he made deliveries
on a rickety blue bicycle
we'd steal more than we could eat

the baker's son had pale red hair
that curled up at the ends
he bled easily and well
I thought he walked by a month ago
but I could not be sure
Heinz says they all look alike

3.

today Heinz wants to taste the black bread
it is crunchy and hard in my mouth
I kiss Heinz and think
death is orange

THE RABBITS

(Ravensbrück, 1944)

For Mme. Vaillant-Couturier, witness,
Nuremberg trials, and others

I remember the pink noses and eyes of the rabbits
kept by the boy from the apartment next door—
small white fur-faces wrinkled, perplexed, as they watched
the world from a cage beneath the courtyard stairs.
When soldiers came for the people in our building,
I hid under the floorboards, came up days later, so thirsty,
and found the building, the courtyard, the street—all empty,
except for the cage where the rabbits lay in death,
their white paws stained as pink as their eyes had once been.
Bloodied from trying to escape, I hoped, from trying
to tear apart the wire and not themselves.

Now they scrape away another piece of me each day,
cells to be examined beneath a glass, more bacilli
to be named, measured, charted. There are no women here,
only an inventory of identical laboratory rodents. My eyes,
once barely blue, swell deeper red with each tear.
I gnaw on memory because it is still mine,
and just close enough to reach.

JOB'S WIFE

For Faye Whitaker

There is a shadow, another end to the story,
a fact remaining: the first ten children are still dead.
I cry for them in our bed at night,
and find myself standing alone
in the old man's fields,
staring toward the distant hills,
toward the high, sacred places,
moving my lips in silence
as I name the names of the lost
and hope that God can't hear me.

RE-MEMBERING

TUBERCULOSIS

1.

a prairie has taken hold in my chest
rattlesnake master   coneflower   big bluestem
stretch themselves in the dark
and scratch against my ribs
a massive root system forming
unbroken blocks of dark soil
damp   waiting for the plow

2.

I could never make the hoop
keep its place around my skinny girl-hips
it dropped to my ankles
no matter how I tried to bump-and-grind
one day I picked it up from the dust of town
and rolled it to the edge of the world
pink plastic turning over on itself
until it became a snake that bit me
smiled   squirmed away laughing
took up its tail in its mouth
and spoke as it revolved out of sight

the snake said
love is like that, girl, sure it is

3.

I did not mean to die for love
but he certainly meant to kill me

when I took my hand away from the knife
there was blood all over the floor
all over the bed   streaked across the faded wallpaper
spotted on the empty bottles lining the dresser top
he began screaming for someone to call the cops
beating on the walls with that familiar fist
his swinging arms slowed   stopped
long before anyone arrived
his breathing heavy   wet   like my own

they pounded and yelled at the door
open up, police but the knife turned into a snake
laughed at me   slithered out an open window
by the time they kicked their way in
the snake was gone   the knife still in my hand
he was just a pile of sod on the floor

4.

the police matron asks a list of questions
in the same bored manner she always uses for me:
have you ever been treated for any of the following?
she pales when I say yes   backs up from the counter
checks a box next to a word
which does not describe
what consumes me

THE MEATPACKER

So here I stand, my face
as white as these coveralls;
spattered with blood, splotched
with a high hangover flush,
a lumpy pudding of fat and gristle
climbing to the tops of my boots.
Anger rustles like a bone sliver
under my fingernail
as I pack more guilt into the vat.
I'm sliding this knife through the beef
while my life swings on me
like a dull cleaver, and the foreman
keeps a vigilant eye on my work.
I tell him I'm throwing clean bones,
but my guts keep getting knotted.

RE-MEMBERING: THE COLOR OF SILENCE

(Bloomington, late June, 1969)

Indiana struggles to breathe;
        there are no lesbians in the Midwest.

Summer dangles like green ties from an apron.
My footsteps are thick on white-edged tile,
and I hear music with no rhythm
clotting inside the walls.

Grease on both sides of my forehead,
amber paste that feels like the sludge
I once packed around a '54 Buick's wheel bearings.

I bite down on plastic, taste metal,
try to lift my head. Wires of light,
a tetragrammaton of silence, connect—
I feel my teeth shouting,
but hear no voices.

Someday I must remember:
        there are no lesbians in the Midwest.

THE ONE-LEGGED MAN STEALS A THREE-LEGGED DOG

1.

Everybody's a comedian.

Sitting up at the bar in Cy's, we saw him walking
down the street, red bandanna tied around his neck
for a collar, sniffing everything, and some joker
yells, *Hey, Jack, there's the dog for you!*
My fists knotted up on their own, but I'd had
too many already to tell for sure
which joker said it.

Still, I watched that dog, black and tan and heavy
through the chest, no pup for sure.
He had a bright retriever face, and as the laughter
petered out around me and the last open-handed
slap echoed off the wooden bar and smoked-up mirror,
I watched that dog move down Main Street
with a hopping grace I've yet to master.
He stopped to piss on a parking meter,
balancing like a circus acrobat on just two legs.
That dog was something—uneven gait and no regret.
So I walked out of the bar in my own
crooked way, and followed that dog.

2.

The bozo with the badge and the flashlight
can hardly keep a straight face.
He thinks I'm kidding when I tell the truth,
so I might as well lie.

I didn't just want the dog; it was more
like I already had him.

Beyond being able to tell if there's rain coming on,
the stump of me turned into some fleshy barometer,
there are these pulsing twitches
that the doctors call phantom pain—the ghost
of a leg, haunting me with cramps.
All it really is, you know, is my leg,
still mine, whispering
I never left. Not really.

And the dog knows how it is,
the voice of what should be gone and isn't,
saying *Come on, boy, run.*
Run on all fours, just as fast as you can.

Believe me, friend, this is not a joke,
it's the truth of all that you thought was cut off:
if it hurts, it's still yours.

THE MERMAID'S DREAM

For Bette Midler

Confusion is a word we know,
though it has no true synonyms—
its nature defies containment.
Passion is not one of our words,
it is one of our moments—
crystalline, immutable,
much more than we had dared hope.

And there is no language this morning,
names neither for my feet nor my love,
no words to describe my hands
aching with what they may not touch,
no explanation for this unshakable knowledge
of a choice forever regretted.

WHY THE DOG HOWLS AT THE MOON

Because it is round, and too large to be swallowed up whole
or to be nudged along the ground; because it is too far away

for her to take huge snapping bites of it; because once her head
is tilted back, sound rolls up great wallops of noise

that bounce from all of her delicate acoustic teeth until each note
rounds itself into an orb, a golden sphere of waves and particles,

ready to tumble across the night in its asteroid-pocked perfection.
Because it is yellow, and she is beyond shouting; because joy

and despair are too large to be held in a small sound,
a small body, a small rock hurtling through space.

Because her heart is broken and comes up from her chest in pieces
that rattle and moan in her throat; because there is no one

to pat her back, to rub her head and sides, to tell her it will one night
be over, that what she will have left after the howling

is the memory of pain and not this musical agony;
because the night demands some sacrifice and she has made it

unselfishly, with her long dog-snout and her great dog-lungs
and her heart, which we all thought unbreakable.

WOMAN WALKING TOWARD HERSELF

For Pamela Bruno, murdered January 21, 1978

1.

This is the mirror in which eyes
become killing stones; sink in,
forget the knife's edge,
and watch ripples spread
over familiar faces.
Somewhere, a woman might scream
until the sound rattles deep.
Here, this silence of blood
keeps falling.

2.

I am under water this morning.

If I look up, I'll see echoes of lovers.
I'll see the bottom of a dinghy
washed paintless by salt water
and ready to drift toward christ.

If I look up, I'll see yesterday afternoon,
when Netty took off her shirt
so the guys could see that her breasts
are bigger than mine.

I have dark beads for fingers.
Count them like tree rings,
and I am twenty-five.
Netty cannot stop laughing.

3.

A woman is walking toward herself.
She makes no sound
as she stops to fill graves with salt
so that the dead may fly away.

Somewhere, a woman is dying,
she is shaving her legs,
she is being born.
Here, blood makes no sound
as it strikes the tile we call *home*.

THE BAKER'S HELPER

Once he's got all the loaves in,
he steps out the back door for a cigarette
and I get left behind to clean.
I can hear him laughing with the guys
from the butcher shop, saying
I'll trade you sourdough for steaks,
while I run soapy water over the hooks.
Some mornings I open the door to the oven
and stand in the blast of hot air.
My face reddens and dries
as I watch the circular route of the shelves
with their pans of bread and rolls.
While they rotate, I imagine another oven,
more ancient, with its three saints and an angel,
and how I always find myself
bowing down to avoid the inferno.

FAT LADIES

1.

Weddings and funerals cast the same pall over the family;
What will we wear? ask the fat ladies, and look
From one to another, sucking our thick lips
To the truest shade of purple, rolling back our eyes
Like worried children. Cotton dresses,
Solid dark colors cut like boxes,
Polyester blend pantsuits with long jackets or vests
To cover dimpled, puckery thighs and buttocks—
Good enough for home, or to stand behind the drugstore counter,
But even fat ladies sense that public occasions demand more.
Our gobbling anxiety deepens to dark-water fear:
At weddings, there are photographs, both posed and candid;
Remember how the lens caught us with jaws wide
To receive a communion of sugar at the eldest cousin's reception?

2.

We are all aunts; we are no one's mother.
Our fat has no person to point at
And say, *If that one hadn't been born. . . .*
We are graceful as only fat ladies can be,
Taking advantage of gravity, allowing
Our soft, serial bellies to move
Independently of she who wears them.
We say, *In the old country, this was wealth,*
Then puff our bready faces to the patio
And stand like bridesmaids around the barbecue grill.

WHAT WE HAD TO DO

For Mary Graves, survivor, Donner Pass, 1847

1.

He said he'd never mention what we had to do,
but I see him watching me in the kitchen,
always asking what's in the pot before he tastes it.
And the children, who have no reason to wonder,
look at me warily over their bowls,
spoons clutched in baby-fat fists.
What they will never know is that it's all food,
everything—trees, oxen, grass, leather—
the only question is what you're willing to eat.

2.

They have wandered away from their food again,
and I fight down my rage, hold back my tongue,
try not to begrudge their chubby legs, their dimpled hands.
I've spent years watching each bite greedily,
counting the drops and spills cleaned from the table,
loading full platters onto the groaning sideboard
and reciting the prayer for the dead under my breath.
Meals are such petty funerals.

NO WITCHES, BUT MADNESS

(Oregon State Mental Hospital, 1970)

The boy with the striped shirt and charcoal pencils
has drawn portraits of the patients, all large eyes
and never a smile, lips taut against any hint
of happiness in this, the green-walled house.
These likenesses are hung with clear tape near the door
where visitors search for the familiar inside the ward.
"They all look crazy" my father mutters,
and my mother shushes him as he adds:
"I hope that kid don't draw a picture of Mom."

But he has drawn her, and my grandmother
has become like all the rest,
a tenant in this boarding house of the lost,
the wanderers along the way.
Grandma, what big eyes you have—eyes full
with what is seen and remains unspoken here
in the mindless stuttering of your talk,
your apologies for everything, even the rain.
I remember seeing a plaque on the lawn
near the state house's bronze pioneer statue:
how our capitol was named for the New England village
where women were killed in communal madness,
and I see my father's blue eyes
glimmering with the flicker of a torch,
see his disappointed mouth
a looped noose.

THE RED-HAIRED WAITRESS

I used to smile with more than teeth.
Sometimes at night I dream these teeth huge,
biting into the hands I feed.
A smile, they tell me, makes the difference
between a clink and a rustle
in the tip jar. So I pull my lips back,
back from these not-so-whites,
remembering what I saw once on cable TV:
how monkeys and dogs grin to threaten,
naked teeth a flashed warning,
a do-not-disturb sign drawing itself with blood.
Watch me smile, friend, and open up your wallet.
Here's a threat you don't even know about.

ANASTASIA

For Anna Anderson

after the bullets the bayonets the fire
when there was nothing left of me
but a spiral of smoke to hold my drifting spirit
I floated above the Siberian plains
on a gust of wind for eternity
moving
      moving
            air in motion

until I came to the young woman
on the bridge her eyes closed nostrils flared out
dreaming of death and resurrection
in that last possible moment
before jumping into the river below
moving
      moving
            water in motion

she drew in her breath as far as she could
I rode in nestled deep in the space
where bubbles hid inside her lungs
in that soft, dark tissue where some air
never leaves always moist and old
moving
      moving
            blood in motion

when she came up from the water
I had given her what all prophets receive
a double portion of my spirit
baptism and resurrection combined
no one knew who I was
      not even she
            who took my name

AFTER MANY YEARS, GRISELDA LOSES PATIENCE

Ne suffreth nat that men yow doon offense.
Chaucer, The Clerk's Tale

Tonight, I saw him watching her again,
our daughter smiling at him as she poured his wine,
and I knew that time had at last wound out its skein:
there is nothing left to give him
but what he has already taken.

Love was never enough. It always fell short
of that thing he names *obedience*. I might call it
something else, something like death,
and fashion my face into a mask.
Tonight, while he sleeps, I'll take the iron from the fire,
I'll strike one blow for each tear swallowed unshed;
one for my tongue, bitten through and bloodied
as I held back from pleading; a blow each for the children
taken from me and returned damaged, no longer mine;
a blow for every prayer ignored by unmerciful Heaven.

Tomorrow, they will not recognize
what I've made of him.

SMALL THINGS

For Gail, dead at 44

There's always a list of what must be done:
details, tasks as mundane as washing the dishes,
carpooling the kids, feeding the horses.
What comfort is it to know that you're needed;
what does it mean to say *They'll miss me when I'm gone?*

This morning, I miss you because of what you'll miss:
the miracle, the moment when time stretches out
like a cat on a windowsill and it all makes sense,
all the light and fur in the world. I miss you
like that, like the gnarled *bonsai* wrapping itself
into the almost-shape of a tree, the small, twisted knot
of what might have been huge.

OPHELIA, DIVING

For Susan Carlson

I tried to write it on the leaves that swirled around me,
but my hands were caught like the large silver fish
I saw captive in the tall water grasses, and so I left no text.

There was no way to tell how it happened; how purple light
became a reminder of all that was lost: father, brother, lover—
well, perhaps lover—all named and still unknown.

The letters wrapped themselves into words on a page
and were still not enough. When the sun began to set,
there was nothing for me to do but to dive

as if I had wax wings to match my wax heart. I was first caught,
then turned within the preternatural spin of the singing spheres;
I was diagrammed in a book once hidden from my sight.

TOURING THE COAST

A BRIEF METAGRAPHIC HISTORY
OF THE OREGON COAST

First, there were tides:
an orchestra of briny water,
fresh, rainy chamber music,
each swelling wave a crescendo
in the waxy ear of God.

Then fire, lashing out
with the frustrated rage
of a rejected lover,
spewing molten rock
wet and hot as a one-night stand.

And wind, grinding its teeth
like a hurried apothecary's pestle;
slinging boulders for buckshot
in the gun of Creation.

TOURING THE COAST

1.

    There's something damp here,
a pool in the center of this marsh,
and I separate the reeds.
    Lover,
let me teach you the language of water,
let your hands, your fingers
become long spades as we go digging for clams
in these tide-shifted flats.

2.

    We shine, you and I,
like this land, a naked O.
We shine like the valley,
lying with her legs spread
and rimmed with radiance,
waiting for summer,
        where in depths of moisture
        there begins a great burning.

3.

     Your face rises above me,
a guardian moon, a dark moon
as constant as the blueback's run.

     What is it to us
if the river changes course?
     If we are unsure,
it is the indecision of the lower Siuslaw,
the sweet brine of an estuary
pulling against itself.

CAPE PERPETUA

For Leslee Freeman

1. From the Stone House

This is the rock, hard as resentment, climbing crag
upon crag to cap those long ribboned southern beaches.
Weathered upthrust, this will stand surrounded by fog-whorls,

obscured by the outline of the sea and the mist rising
from sea itself. Persistent Scotch broom clings to the hillside,
flourishing in salty hardship, sandblown half-naked,

bare on the windside and bent against the mountain.
This is the rock, defiant postern of silence,
an illusion of power, a rogue, a geologic fist

clenched in the face of the constant, victorious sea.

2. From the Trail

In here, air rings with memory—misery whips pulled back
and forth in rhythm whined between wet slices of wood,
resonated against the pith like fiddles in a Triple-C camp.

Half-light here. The soil never dries—it sinks beneath our feet
as if rotted. We take our bearings by witch's hair, by orange-edged
fungus protruding from spruce stumps; we ignore the moss

as it ignores the sun. This dampness feels welcome;
rain refuses to soak in and forms beads on the rusty underside
of licorice fern. This is the underbelly, a little truce

between bursts of fire, the silence at the core of being.

THE NATURE OF HUMILITY, AS EXPLAINED
BY SEAGULLS

For Cathy, on her birthday

If the sky,
        having tired of endlessly
                holding down the sea,
should choose to fall,
        we could not stop it.
                If the beach could not remain
stretched out like a languid cat,
        but found some deep, demanding need
                to coil up, tightening itself
back to the beginning,
        we could not stop it.

        We could not stop it
with our cacophonous, raging curses,
        our screeched Pentecostal prayer-wails.
                Some things will not change for us,
so we must change for them:
        this is the Law of Flight.

One gray tipfeather lifted before
the face of the breeze
and we glide on the weighted
motion of air,
but all the power-filled sweeps
of these blessed wings
cannot bank a turn
into the roiling countenance of hurricanes.
Control is beyond us;
it is the prerogative of storms.
We must land or die, slightly discontent
in the knowledge that flight
is greater than any bird.

LINSLAW CUTOFF

1.

Billy went into the woods
sweating beneath the pines
He got pitch on his hands
until it wouldn't wash off

It was a damp day
The murdering wind
loosed a widowmaker
and he never even saw it coming

2.

Bill Senior talked with his son
at five-thirty breakfasts
through salt and pepper whiskers
Billy listened to every egg-coated word

Watch out when the moss gets dry
hangs brown and thirsty
like a noose from the gallows

The same day that Billy started high school
Bill Senior went into the woods
where a choke cable snapped loose in the wind
When the log crashed down
it cracked both his hard-hat
and his head wide open
He bled to death in the back of a pickup truck
down in Otter Slough

3.

Billy's dead
on a muddy logging road
sixteen miles east
of the Linslaw cutoff

His metallic blood paints the bed
of the grimy yellow pickup
It glints in shafts of light
as the sun dies with him
impaled on pines

The old man kneeling beside him
leans back to relieve his monstrous belly
He stubs his cigar on the tirewell
pounds on the window with a greasy fist

You can slow down, Jackie
it's too late

SPENT SHELLS

Grampa Chuck and Uncle Buck and Daddy
stand in a row on the crest of the riverbank
shooting four-tens at seagulls.
It's like something from the late movie;
a firing squad lined up for blood and glory,
and the birds explode with each blast
into guts and feathers, as shotgun reports
echo across the valley.

Chucky and I collect the shell casings—
some red, some blue, with crisp brass bottoms.
Now we have armies. Line them up on the grass,
knock them over with pine cones. I'm American,
and I hold four dead Vietnamese in my hand.

A seal has made its way upriver.
Small and black, it scrounges for fish
amid the wreckage of Sunday.
Uncle Buck and Daddy fire in unison,
the seal floats for three brief beats,
then sinks into the dull green river.
They laugh, load up again, call for more beer.

DIGGING FOR CLAMS

For Jane

1.

This is the truth of mud:
black and clinging
fresh from the estuary
a pungent smell sitting
on the back of my tongue
like an old secret
a neighborly fear
the one bad habit
that refuses to break
It's a difficult business
this attempt
to pry clams open—
they had best be boiled
until they surrender
some honest flesh

2.

Look for air holes
then cut in with the
spade
and push down
Lean hard on the handle
back straining
laboring
uncovering:

red-faced, sweating,
each shovel full of black mud
and sand—riverdweller's
camouflage—slapping
to the left side, blind side
A flash of shell
as the clam squirts thick water
propelling itself
away from me
from the light
from this world

ANOTHER GUILTY LITTLE POEM

My hands have become huge
in the insulated oven mitts
as I place a drip-dry casserole
on the counter to cool
next to a paint-by-numbers pie.
I remember what my momma used to say:
how convenience and quality
are not the same, how the good
is often the enemy of the best.
Momma, you're not here,
but I can recite without prompting
a list of thou-shalt-nots
as long as a rubbery noodle.
There's always something to be homesick for:
mossy Oregon rain,
the smell of clam chowder
simmering in the kitchen,
the day I saw all the guilt in the world
in a crumpled-up package
of chocolate chips.

DURING THE FLOOD

I am born when the rain comes
and does not stop.
The river rises like uncaged sparrows,
covers pastures and gravel roads,
pulls rowboats from their moorings,
carries my father to the bay.
Steelhead float downstream,
silver bellies rocking with the current.

DADDY WAS A GREASER

Before the town had traffic lights, he'd wait
until we had crossed the bridge
then he'd gun it up Glenada Hill
like a true V-8 bandit,
rapping the glasspacks extra loud
as we blazed past Our Lady of the Dunes.
My mother would whine, he'd laugh—
reciting the catechism
of a Honduras maroon SuperSport,
knowing his life was as sacred
as a snapped axle.

CROSSING THE BAR

Harbor seals are small black dots around the Coast Guard dory
as it rides over the bar. The seals are surfing today,

defiant as they arch their backs and glide belly-down on the breakers.
They pass close to the rocks—we wait, half-expecting

to see one shatter red against the jetty and drop into the frothy channel.
But they don't miss, these seals—they aim true and from the open sea,

slide effortlessly across the bar and into the river, flippers
pulling drag on the current: a single foamy moment.

GOING HOME, AFTER YEARS AWAY

Siuslaw Bay, Oregon, September 1994

The dock felt like it rocked beneath us; the gray-green
water churned below the surface, flashing white or dull silver

as the salmon ran upriver. Auntie Peg would laugh and say,
Usta be you could walk across the river on their backs.

She'd lower the motor of her boat gently, ease into the channel,
adding her presence to the dotted pattern of sporting boats

like measles on the water from the jetty to that place, miles inland,
where the water narrowed and shallowed into a cold, rocky creek.

She is dead now fifteen years and the river is empty, neither boats
nor fish, nothing to break up the empty space but the dark skeletons

of abandoned fish traps. On the radio, sportsmen, boat owners
and native peoples all argue about who will cast the last line,

who will land the last Chinook. Old-timers shake their heads,
lay blame, remain as confused as the harbor seals that sun themselves

on sandbars, puzzled by this chronic hunger.

ABOUT THE AUTHOR

Kel Munger was born and raised on the Oregon coast, and moved to Iowa in 1978 to attend Drake University. She left Drake before receiving a degree and worked at several jobs in central Iowa, many of which have become topics of her poems. In 1987, she joined the Ames, Iowa, Police Department, initially working as a parking enforcement officer before being promoted to 911-Dispatcher/Jailer in 1989. While working full-time, she completed a Bachelor's Degree in English at Iowa State University, graduating in May of 1995.

Munger was the selected as the 1995-96 Pearl M. Hogrefe Fellow in Creative Writing at Iowa State University, and resigned from the police department to work full-time on a Master's Degree in Literature, which she received in May 1997. She recently moved to Columbia, Missouri, where she lives with her partner and their dog, Bette.